Ladybird  Readers

ROALD DAHL

The Enormous Crocodile
Activity Book

Based on the original title by Roald Dahl
Illustrated by Quentin Blake

Written by Hazel Geatches
Song lyrics on page 16 written by Wardour Studios

Singing *	Reading	Speaking	Critical thinking
Spelling	Writing	Listening *	

Match the words to the pictures.

1 bench

2 bite

3 jungle

4 see-saw

5 fair

6 tail

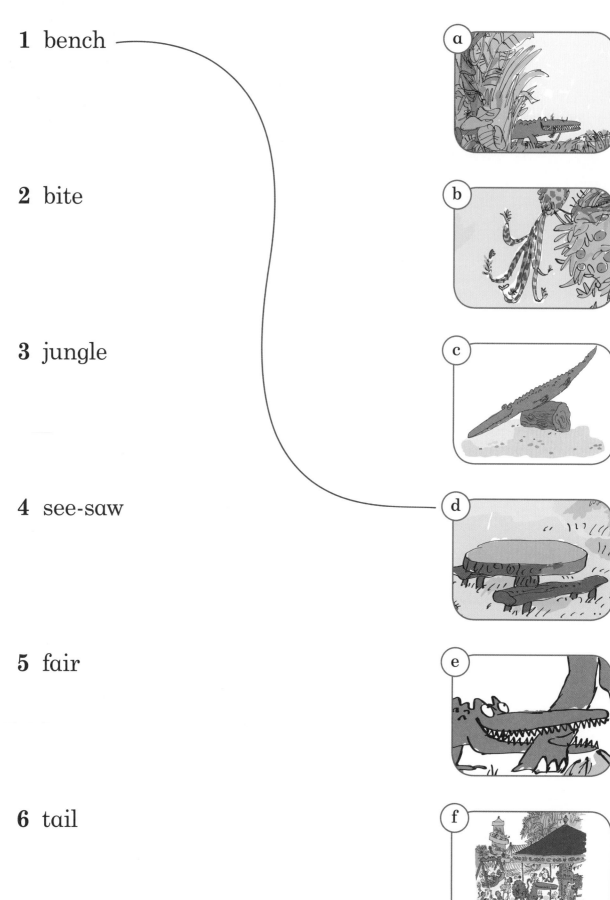

a

b

c

d

e

f

2 Look, match, and write the words.

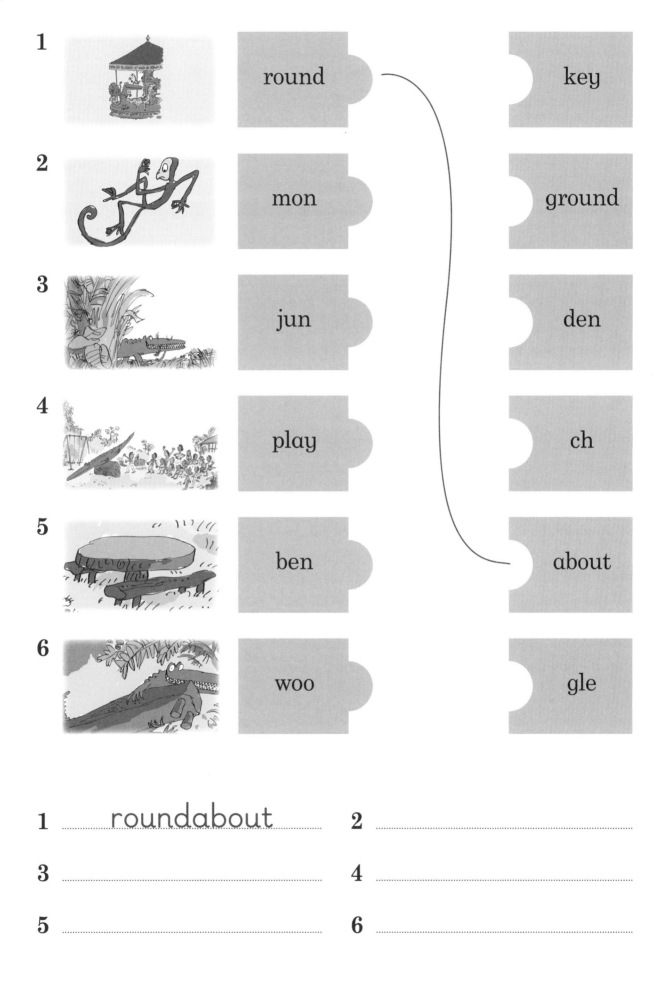

1
round — key

2
mon — ground

3
jun — den

4
play — ch

5
ben — about

6
woo — gle

1 ..... roundabout

2 .....

3 .....

4 .....

5 .....

6 .....

"I want to go on that horse!" said a girl.

"I want to go on that old wooden crocodile," said a boy.

Then, the Roly-Poly Bird flew down. "It isn't a wooden crocodile," he said. "It's the Enormous Crocodile, and he wants to eat you!"

The children ran from the Enormous Crocodile.

30
31

1 "I want to go on that old wooden crocodile." b

2 "It isn't a wooden crocodile." ....

3 "He wants to eat you!" ....

4 "I want to go on that horse!" ....

5 "It's the Enormous Crocodile." ....

*To complete this activity, listen to track 2 of the Reader audio download available at **www.ladybirdeducation.co.uk**

4 **Look and read.**
Write the correct words on the lines.

> see-saw   roundabout   flowers   tail

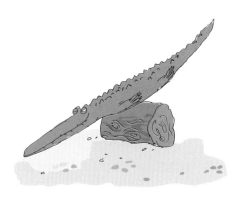

1 The children were
excited when they
saw the new
_____see-saw_____.

2 Trunky held the
Enormous Crocodile's
_____.

3 There were
_____
on the table.

4 The Enormous
Crocodile stood on the
_____
at the fair.

5 Read, color, and draw.

1 There is a horse on the roundabout. Color the horse black.

2 Next to the horse there is a lion. Color it yellow.

3 Can you see the slide? Color it purple.

4 Behind the fair is the jungle. Color it green.

5 Now, draw a bird on top of the roundabout.

6 Do the crossword.

Down

1 The Enormous Crocodile bit the Roly-Poly Bird's . . . .

2 "I have clever . . . ," said the Enormous Crocodile.

3 There were two of these in the big, brown river.

4 Crocodiles can swim here.

Across

3 The Enormous Crocodile wanted to eat one for lunch.

4 The Enormous Crocodile stood on this at the fair.

5 There are lots of animals and plants here.

7 Work with a friend.

Ask and answer questions about the picture.

1 Which animal is in the picture?

A crocodile.

2 Where are the flowers?

3 How many children are there?

4 What do the children want to do?

8 Draw a picture of the Enormous Crocodile.
Read the questions and write about
the Enormous Crocodile. 📖 ✏️ ❓

1 What's your name?

My name is the Enormous Crocodile.

2 Where do you live?

3 What do you eat?

4 What are your ideas?

Listen, and circle the correct words. *

1 (crocodile)/ crocodiles

2 leg / legs

3 foot / feet

4 flower / flowers

5 tree / trees

6 child / children

*To complete this activity, listen to track 3 of the Reader audio download available at **www.ladybirdeducation.co.uk**

10 Circle the correct pictures.

1 Where do the crocodiles live?

ⓐ  ⓑ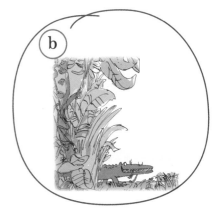

2 Who wants to eat a child for lunch?

ⓐ ⓑ

3 Who lives in a tree?

ⓐ ⓑ

4 Who goes to school?

ⓐ ⓑ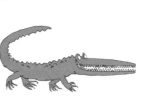

5 Who can fly?

ⓐ ⓑ

11 Find the words.

b	m	o	k	e	y	q	a	b	m	g	t
j	u	n	t	s	m	o	n	k	e	y	a
u	e	j	u	b	n	j	r	b	a	n	g
r	b	u	o	i	p	q	a	a	e	n	s
o	i	n	e	r	g	u	r	w	w	a	t
u	t	g	n	d	t	w	b	f	a	i	r
n	e	l	g	a	v	o	j	o	i	o	i
t	h	e	t	w	s	o	b	e	n	c	h
a	e	a	x	k	w	d	z	d	s	e	e
i	r	o	u	n	d	a	b	o	u	t	s
l	o	n	a	n	t	l	o	k	e	r	e
e	e	y	e	h	g	e	i	f	c	h	n

bird

bang

roundabout

bite

wood

bench

tail

monkey

fair

jungle

12

12 Look at the letters. Write the words.

1

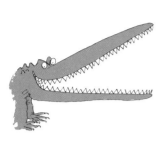

> u s r o m e o n

The crocodile was

_____ enormous _____.

2

> r y n g u h

He went to the playground because he was

_____.

3

> t i e l l t

He wanted to catch a nice

_____ child.

4

> t h a r t s i g

He got on the wood and stayed very

_____.

5

> c i x d e e t

The children were _____

when they came out of school.

Read, and circle the correct words.

1

The crocodile (swam)/ swim across the river.

2

In the jungle, the crocodile **meet** / **met** Trunky, the elephant.

3

The crocodile **bit** / **bite** Trunky on the leg.

4

The crocodile bit the Roly-Poly Bird's tail, but the bird **fly** / **flew** out of the tree.

14 Work with a friend. Talk about the two pictures.
How are they different?

a

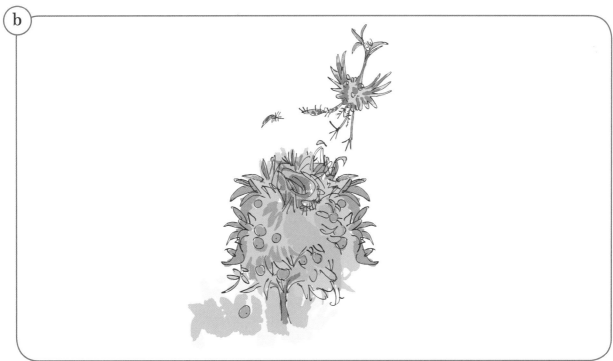

b

> *In picture a, the animal is big.*
> *In picture b, the animal is small.*

15 Sing the song.

The Enormous Crocodile, no, no, no!
Where do you think he can go, go, go?
He thinks he can eat you!
He doesn't know what Trunky can do!

"I have clever ideas,"
says the Enormous Crocodile.
"I have clever ideas. I want to eat a child."
Muggle-Wump says, "No!
Children, you must go!
Crocodile, you must stop!"

"I have clever ideas,"
says the Enormous Crocodile.
"I have clever ideas. I want to eat a child."
Trunky says, "No!
Children, you must run!"
Trunky throws Crocodile into the sun.

The Enormous Crocodile, no, no, no!
Where do you think he can go, go, go?
He thinks he can eat you!
He doesn't know what Trunky can do!

 *To complete this activity, listen to track 4 of the Reader audio download available at www.ladybirdeducation.co.uk